Becoming a Neighboring Church

COMPANION STUDY AND LAUNCH GUIDE

By Rick Rusaw, Brian Mavis,
Krista Petty, and Allen White

"LEADERS HAVE ONLY TWO TOOLS AT THEIR DISPOSAL: WHAT THEY SAY AND HOW THEY ACT. WHAT THEY SAY MIGHT BE INTERESTING, BUT HOW THEY ACT IS ALWAYS CRUCIAL."

—Alan Deutschman, *Walk the Walk: The #1 Rule for Real Leaders*

Table of Contents

Message from the Authors

This guide is designed especially for church leadership teams desiring to elevate the value of loving your neighbor as yourself within the congregation and community. As leaders of neighboring in your church, part of the task is the systems and strategies, but a greater part of the task is setting the example for neighboring yourselves.

Why a guide for leaders? Dave Runyon and Jay Pathak, co-authors of *The Art of Neighboring*, have led hundreds of churches into neighboring with some churches embedding neighboring into their DNA and others not. In preparing to write *The Neighboring Church*, we talked with them to glean more insights into working with church leaders and creating a neighboring ethos (not just a neighboring program that lives and dies). Dave shared, "Everything rises and falls on leadership. It would be hard to overstate the importance of the lead pastor and the staff making a commitment to engage their own neighborhoods. The only leadership that is sustainable is leadership by example. Practically speaking, senior leadership teams that fail to learn their neighbors' names seldom see long-term results."

So, we see the leadership in neighboring as a cornerstone and want to equip you to have meaningful and challenging conversations as a staff, an eldership, a leadership team...whatever the church's leadership design or size. That is one of the beautiful things about obedience to the Great Commandment: it doesn't matter what size, place, culture or context in which you find yourself leading. Neighboring is comprehensive and a big deal to God. He loves the neighbors.

In His Service,
Krista Petty, Resource Editor
Rick Rusaw & Brian Mavis, Co-Authors

How to Use This Companion Study

This discussion guide helps the Leadership Team facilitate discussion based on their reading of *The Neighboring Church* book. While the book will inspire the team, the companion study will help the team examine the churche's values, integrate the values of neighboring, and practice neighboring in their own neighborhoods.

The Companion Study follows the sections of *The Neighboring Church* book: Introduction, Chapters 1-6, and Conclusion. Read the corresponding section BEFORE the Leadership Team meeting.

EACH LESSON IN THE COMPANION STUDY IS MADE UP OF SEVERAL PARTS:

Something to Think About

The section is a short introduction to the discussion topic for each of the eight lessons in the companion study. Ask someone on the leadership team to read this section aloud to the team.

Something to Talk About

This section contains five or so questions about the topic. It's best to have a copies of *The Neighboring Church* handy as a reference for this section. This discussion will be successful if each team member is given permission to speak freely in the meeting. Neighboring has implications not only in neighborhoods, but also in the vision, structure, and priorities of the church itself. Every member of the leadership team will have a vested interest in their department, so it is essential for each person to have their say in the team meetings, since everyone has something at stake.

Watch the Video

The video component for each lesson contains stories from practitioners in the neighboring movement who will inspire the team. The team will gain perspective in neighboring by hearing from these voices.

Something to Act Upon

This is where the rubber meets the road. The Leadership Team is not only responsible for casting vision and leading the way in neighboring, but must also live a neighboring life themselves. Who are your neighbors? How has God called you to serve them? Effective Neighboring Life launches are lead by leaders who are walking the walk.

Sermon/Lesson Idea

Each lesson of the Companion Study ends with suggestions for preaching a sermon or teaching a lesson on neighboring based on the principles in the chapter. This section is made up of a Scripture Text, Main Idea, Illustration, and Actions Points. These are suggestions for the basis of a future sermon or lesson in your church that could align with *The Neighboring Life* launch.

Introduction to The Neighboring Church

Something to Think About

"What do we mean by 'organic' when it is used in Christian circles? It first means being present with a community, with neighbors, with a particular social group or subculture—not nearby, but within. It means listening to and watching, growing to understand the assets and needs of a community, its opportunities and problems. All that implies building relationships, and potentially unexpected partnerships. It is not without agenda, all relationships have an agenda. It is not simply sitting around and waiting. It requires effort, but a different kind of effort than typically exerted by Christian leaders. Why is this ministry of presence necessary? Because an "organic" approach presumes that God is already present and at work within any given context. That context, whatever it may be, has the raw tools already in place for its transformation. There are leaders, assets, resources and solutions right there. The question for the Christian leader is whether or not they will pay attention close enough, then build relationships of love and trust that might nurture those gifts already present."

**—from Jason Evans, Organic Vs. Organized,
blog.digitaljasonevans.com**

Something to Talk About

1. Which word would best describe your church: organized or organic?

    _____

    _____

    _____

    _____

2. What are the benefits of being organized? Of being organic?

    _____

    _____

    _____

    _____

3. What are the potential pitfalls of each one: organized and organic?

    _____

    _____

    _____

    _____

    _____

4. Have you ever come to a point where you thought your faith would be better off without the church, like Brian and Julie did?

_____

_____

_____

_____

_____

_____

5. Ramin Razavi said, "Structure is not a creator, but it can be an accelerant." How have you seen this to be true?

_____

_____

_____

_____

_____

_____

Watch the Video

The video contains stories from neighboring churches across North America. Let these testimonies inspire you in neighboring your community.

Something to Act Upon

1. Make a list of the church's current structures.

    _____

    _____

2. How do the structures foster environments where natural relationships grow and flourish? What could be improved?

    _____

    _____

3. How could the church's structures inhibit relationships between neighbors?

    _____

    _____

4. Read Chapter 1 of *The Neighboring Church* to prepare for the next meeting.

Sermon/Lesson Idea

Text: Isaiah 43:18, 19; Mark 2:22

MAIN IDEA

Where has the church gotten stuck? Are we willing to recognize a new thing when it comes upon us? "Jesus said we need new wineskins, not no wineskins."

"Spirit-led people never stop growing and changing and recognizing the new moment of opportunity. How strange to think that so much of religion became worship of the status quo and a neurotic fear of failure." —Richard Rohr

Illustration

The Lab or the Factory by Seth Godin (page 22, *The Neighboring Church*)

Action Points

Starting over. If you moved to a new town and discovered you were the only Christ-follower in this new place, what would be the first things you would do to build a faith community? What would it look like to make disciples? Draw a model of what you would do. Are you doing those things now? If not, what's stopping you?

Chapter 1:
What Matters Most

Something to Think About

"Once upon a time there was a colony of ants who were busy doing whatever ants do with their lives. God wanted to tell the ants of His love for them and His eternal home prepared for them. What was the very best way for God to communicate to those ants? The only possible way to speak to the ants was to become an ant and speak their language. So he did, and they believed."

—from Jim Burns, One Life: 50 Powerful Devotions for Students

Something to Talk About

1. How many households are represented in your congregation?

   _____

   _____

   _____

   _____

2. If each household reached out to get to know the 8 neighbors around them, how many households would that be?

   _____

   _____

   _____

   _____

3. If you take the number of households and multiply that by 2.5 (average household size), what is the congregation's potential impact for loving the neighbors?

   _____

   _____

   _____

   _____

4. What percentage of the congregation's resources of time, talent and money go toward the worship experiences or church programs?

    _____

    _____

    _____

    _____

5. What would it look like for the church to be less program-centric and more scattered out into neighborhoods?

    _____

    _____

    _____

    _____

6. Brainstorm ways to infuse teaching on neighboring into the current programs, classes or series.

    _____

    _____

    _____

    _____

Watch the Video

The video contains stories from neighboring churches across North America. Let these testimonies inspire you in neighboring your community.

Something to Act Upon

1. One of the tools in neighboring is the Block Map. Start filling in everything you know about the neighbors surrounding you: their names, occupations, hopes, dreams or hurts.

DO YOU KNOW YOUR NEIGHBORS' NAMES, HISTORY, HOPES AND HURTS?

_____ _____ _____

_____ _____ _____

_____ _____ _____

_____ _____

_____ **YOU** _____

_____ _____

_____ _____ _____

_____ _____ _____

_____ _____ _____

2. Share with each other what you know and pray for the neighbors.

    _____

    _____

    _____

3. Read Chapter 2 of *The Neighboring Church* to prepare for the next meeting.

Sermon/Lesson Idea

Text: John 1:14 and John 13:34-35

MAIN IDEA

Motivated by love, Jesus came to us. Likewise, followers of Christ must be motivated by the love of Christ to show love to our neighbors. Love, inspired by the Holy Spirit, may be the only thing our neighbors will take notice of in our distracted and cynical world. Jesus promises that love would be the identifying mark of a Christian.

Illustration

Are we doing what Jesus said matters most? A loving neighbor is better than a good program. Share Brian's story of the city calling to mow a neighbor's yard. (page 5-7, *The Neighboring Church*)

Action Points

Who do you love more today than you did a year ago? How are you showing that you are growing in love of God and the neighbors?

Chapter 2:
Love God,
Love Your Neighbor

Something to Think About

"Before we can deeply love our neighbors as ourselves, we need to learn to love God with our lives. And the way to love him is to obey him."
—*The Neighboring Church*, **page 30.**

"It is not enough to say yes to the truth of love and then ignore the way of love. Love should move us closer to others."
—*The Neighboring Church*, **page 33.**

Something to Talk About

1. Have you ever thought of loving the neighbor as an act of obedience? How does that change things?

   _____

   _____

   _____

   _____

   _____

   _____

2. What holds people back or distracts people from loving their neighbors?

   _____

   _____

   _____

   _____

   _____

   _____

3. The early followers were called people of "The Way," not people of the experience, the right doctrine, moral values, or even people of the church? What would you call followers in the faith community today?

_____

_____

_____

_____

_____

_____

4. Make a list of some of the possible outcomes to people being faithful to loving their neighbors. What might change in the community if that began to happen?

_____

_____

_____

_____

_____

_____

Watch the Video

The video contains stories from neighboring churches across North America. Let these testimonies inspire you in neighboring your community.

Something to Act Upon

1. Satan tempts us to be non-serving, non-suffering, and non-relational, just like he did Jesus in the desert. The Jesus way is to move in close. How can you move in closer to loving the neighbors?

   _____

   _____

   _____

2. What sacrifices will it take? Write it down and ask God to show you the way.

   _____

   _____

   _____

3. Read Chapter 3 of *The Neighboring Church* to prepare for the next meeting.

Sermon/Lesson Idea

Text: Mark 12:28-31, Deuteronomy 6:4-9, Leviticus 19:18

MAIN IDEA

Jesus was challenged to find the vital verse—the key command—that got to the essence of scripture and the heart of God's will. In Mark, Jesus begins the Great Commandment by quoting the Shema, three sections in scripture faithful Jews memorized and repeated twice daily. It was like their pledge of allegiance to the one and only God. Jesus also quotes Deuteronomy 6:5, saying we are to love God with all our heart, soul and strength. God is not commanding a feeling, but rather action and loyalty. Jesus concludes the commandment with "Love the neighbor as yourself," meaning, love the neighbor who is like you.

Illustration

If you asked your son to mow the lawn and he didn't move, you might ask him again. You will know he heard you when he shows you he heard you by actually mowing the lawn. Hearing isn't merely auditory. It is also about obedience.

Action Points

List all the ways you are like your neighbors and share that with someone. Pray that God will reveal even more truths about the things you and your neighbor have in common.

Chapter 3:
Being a Good Neighbor is Better Than a Good Program

Something to Think About

"Neighboring is not another church program to implement. We must take the approach that we are going to do this until our city leaders say Christians are the best neighbors in their city. This is the prime imperative of God, and we keep living this until it is the normative behavior of every Christian."
—*The Neighboring Church*, page 49.

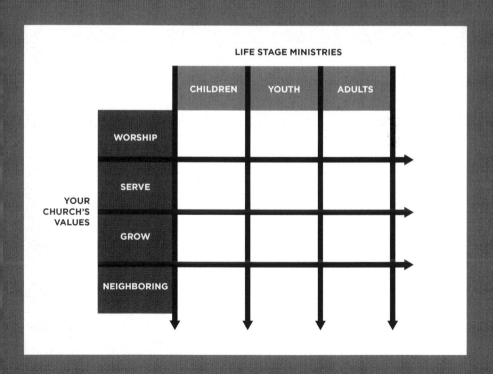

Something to Talk About

1. What are your church's values?

   _____

   _____

   _____

   _____

   _____

   _____

2. Do your values flow throughout every ministry area of the church?

   _____

   _____

   _____

   _____

   _____

   _____

   _____

3. Oak Hills Church, featured in this chapter, is organized by Campus Life and Community Life. LifeBridge Church is organized by values and life stage ministries. How is your church organized? Draw a model of it.

4. Spend some time brainstorming how neighboring could become part of the flow.

    _____

    _____

    _____

    _____

    _____

    _____

    _____

Watch the Video

The video contains stories from neighboring churches across North America. Let these testimonies inspire you in neighboring your community.

Something to Act Upon

1. Are you a Belong, Grow or Serve person? (see page 59, *The Neighboring Church*)

    _____

    _____

    _____

2. Think of a way to use your strength in loving your neighbors and leading the church to as well.

    _____

    _____

    _____

3. Read Chapter 4 of *The Neighboring Church* to prepare for the next meeting.

Sermon/Lesson Idea

Text: Matthew 22:36-40, Matthew 25:30-46; Matthew 28:18-20

MAIN IDEA

Become a church that does what matters most by obeying the Great Commandment (to love God and our neighbor, Matthew 22:36-40), The Great Compassion (to serve the least, Matthew 25:31-46) and the Great Commission (to make disciples, Matthew 28:18-20). How are each of these anchor points in scripture represented in the life of the church?

Illustration

Keep the motives in check. Don't let anything hijack the endgame. (see illustration, page 48, *The Neighboring Church*)

Action Points

How can we take what we have been doing in our ministry on campus and flow it out into homes and neighborhoods?

Chapter 4:
Who is My Neighbor?

Something to Think About

"I don't know if loving my neighbors has been good for them, but I know it's been good for me."
—**Brian Mavis, *The Neighboring Church***

Something to Talk About

1. How can loving your neighbor serve as an action to mature and grow yourself spiritually?

    _____

    _____

    _____

    _____

    _____

    _____

2. We don't just love the neighbors we choose but the ones God chooses for us. Why do you think God may have chosen the particular neighbors to live near you?

    _____

    _____

    _____

    _____

    _____

    _____

3. Brainstorm ways you can share stories of neighboring. What communication channels could you use? Who can collect and distribute these stories?

_____

_____

_____

_____

_____

_____

_____

_____

_____

_____

_____

_____

Watch the Video

The video contains stories from neighboring churches across North America. Let these testimonies inspire you in neighboring your community.

Something to Act Upon

1. Sketch out your own life and maturity in Christ. What were some of the significant catalysts for growth?

    _____

    _____

    _____

2. When were there seasons that threw you for a loop and what was the outcome?

    _____

    _____

    _____

3. Read Chapter 5 of *The Neighboring Church* to prepare for the next meeting.

Sermon/Lesson Idea

Text: Luke 10:30-37; Luke 6:32-24

MAIN IDEA

When Jesus issued the Great Commandment, he invited us to expand our relationships and, in turn, build our character. Neighboring is quite possibly the best spiritual formation process a church can initiate. The Good Samaritan is an example.

Illustration

Love is Loopy. How do we act when we become disoriented, when life gets turned upside down? (see illustration below & pages 78-79, *The Neighboring Church*)

Action Points

Imagine who would be the hardest person for you to love. Now, imagine Jesus loving that person. What does that look like?

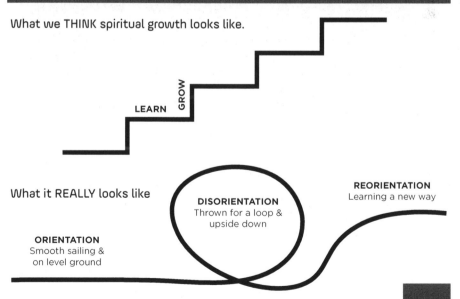

What we THINK spiritual growth looks like.

LEARN GROW

What it REALLY looks like

ORIENTATION
Smooth sailing &
on level ground

DISORIENTATION
Thrown for a loop &
upside down

REORIENTATION
Learning a new way

Chapter 5:
The Practices of
Neighboring

Something to Think About

"Who's been sitting around your
dinner table?"
—Nate Bush, *The Neighboring Church*,
page 105.

Something to Talk About

1. How long have you lived in your current neighborhood?

    _____

    _____

    _____

    _____

2. What things cause you to cocoon and to make you less social?

    _____

    _____

    _____

    _____

3. What do you talk about at leadership/staff meetings? How could you infuse neighboring into those conversations consistently?

    _____

    _____

    _____

    _____

4. Brainstorm 10 creative questions your church members can ask their neighbors (that go beyond What's your name? How are you? and What do you do for a living?).

1. _____

2. _____

3. _____

4. _____

5. _____

6. _____

7. _____

8. _____

9. _____

10. _____

Watch the Video

The video contains stories from neighboring churches across North America. Let these testimonies inspire you in neighboring your community.

Something to Act Upon

1. Pick a neighbor to begin praying for. Write your neighbors name here:

    _____

2. Pray that God will help you want to love this neighbor and will show you how he wants them to be loved.

3. Read Chapter 6 of *The Neighboring Church* to prepare for the next meeting.

Sermon/Lesson Idea

Text: Ephesians 1:18; 1 Timothy 2:1; 2 Corinthians 5:16-20

MAIN IDEA

Open a window into your brain and begin to see things you didn't before. Prayer does that.

Illustration

Activate the reticular activator. (see page 97, *The Neighboring Church*)

Action Points

Pray for yourself, that God would help you see your neighbors and help you see where God is already at work in their lives and in the entire neighborhood. Pray for your neighbors. Pray small specific prayers. Pray for the willingness to be the answer when you can.

The practices of neighboring
STAY | PRAY | PLAY | SAY

Chapter 6:
What Not to Do and
What to Do Instead

Something to Think About

"Jesus didn't say to love our neighbors as ourselves so that we can fix them, get them on our team, or make them better neighbors. He simply said: Love your neighbor as yourself."
—*The Neighboring Church*, **page 125**

Something to Talk About

1. What steps could be taken to greater align everyone to the vision of neighboring?

    _____

    _____

    _____

    _____

2. Is there margin in your life and in the life of your church so that people can be present in their neighborhoods to love their neighbors?

    _____

    _____

    _____

    _____

3. What objections might people have to moving to a more neighborhood-centric model of ministry?

    _____

    _____

    _____

    _____

4. How will you, with unity, answer those objections?

_____

_____

_____

_____

_____

5. How much are you willing to invest in neighboring as a church? (example: amount of time teaching on it; amount of communication given to it; amount of staff time, money and resources to living it, promoting it, and developing it)

_____

_____

_____

_____

_____

_____

_____

Watch the Video

The video contains stories from neighboring churches across North America. Let these testimonies inspire you in neighboring your community.

Something to Act Upon

1. Identify the people who could be neighboring champions. Write their names here:

    _____

    _____

    _____

    _____

    _____

    _____

2. Imagine what a neighboring team could do to infuse neighboring into the DNA of the church.

3. Read the Conclusion of *The Neighboring Church* to prepare for the next meeting.

Sermon/Lesson Idea

Text: John 5:17, 19-20; Ephesians 5:15-16

MAIN IDEA

Learn to depend on God, like Jesus did, and make the most of every opportunity. Pray, wait and watch.

Illustration

Live a Kairos Life (see page 142, "Do What the Father is Doing", *The Neighboring Church*)

Action Points

Pick a day of the week to walk the neighborhood and pray. Rather than trying to make something happen, wait to see how God answers your prayers. Wait with a sense of expectation. Finally, pay attention and be ready for the opportunities God presents, because he will place them before you.

Conclusion: Thousands of Small Stories and a Few Big Ones

Something to Think About

"It was he who gave some to be apostles, some to be prophets, some to be evangelists, and some to be pastors and teachers to prepare God's people for works of service, so that the body of Christ may be built up until we all reach unity in the faith and in the knowledge of the Son of God and become mature, attaining to the whole measure of the fullness of Christ.

"Then we will no longer be infants, tossed back and forth by the waves and blown here and there by every wind of teaching and by the cunning and craftiness of men in their deceitful scheming. Instead, speaking the truth in love, we will in all things grow up into him who is the head, that is, Christ. From him, the whole body, joined and held together by every supporting ligament grows and builds itself up in love, as each part does its work."
—Ephesians 4: 11-15

Something to Talk About

1. Every good church leadership team needs a balance of voices at the table. What is the make-up of your team, considering the above scripture as a guide?

_____

_____

_____

_____

_____

_____

2. What are your team's strengths?

_____

_____

_____

_____

_____

_____

3. Where are your team's weaknesses?

_____

_____

_____

_____

4. Do the interactions and conversations with one another focus more on transformation or transactions?

_____

_____

_____

_____

5. As you move deeper into neighboring, how will each of you protect the neighboring ethos?

_____

_____

_____

_____

_____

Watch the Video

The video contains stories from neighboring churches across North America. Let these testimonies inspire you in neighboring your community.

Something to Act Upon

1. Brainstorm ways each of you as a member of the church leadership team can be a good neighbor to the residents, businesses, and organizations located closest to the church building or meeting location.

    _____

    _____

    _____

2. Now brainstorm about the people of the congregation and who has gifts that could be put into action, helping you to follow through on some of the ways the church can be a good neighbor to the people around you.

    _____

    _____

    _____

Sermon/Lesson Idea

Text: 1 Peter 2:9-12; Zechariah 8:23

MAIN IDEA

Our collective representation of Christ can change the world. Neighboring gets us to the concept of actually living out the priesthood of believers, being light on our streets.

Illustration

"Imagine what it would look like for every Christian to follow the Great Commandment literally." (page 161-162, Dan Simpson's story, *The Neighboring Church*)

Action Points

Post a map of the community in the church lobby. Ask people to mark or pin their street on the map and find another family that lives close the them. Join together to pray for the specific area of the city.

the
neighboring
life

Launch Guide

Introduction to The Neighboring Life

In giving the Great Commandment, Jesus said, "And the second is like it: 'Love your neighbor as yourself'" (Matthew 22:39).

Yes, Love Your Literal Neighbor

A "neighbor" in the scriptures is best defined as anyone in close proximity to you that has need. By that definition, anyone could be your neighbor. Unfortunately, many of us use that wide definition of neighbor, then go on to pick and choose who we are going to love and who we are not going to love. We take matters into our hands based on our preferences or conveniences, which was never Jesus' intention.

Jesus' example to us was being fully present wherever he went. He paid attention and met the needs of the people right in front of him. Later, Jesus' encouragement to the disciples as he first sent them out was to start loving people right where they were. They were to start the mission in Jerusalem before they took the message any further (Acts 1:8). In the same way, we cannot neglect the people right next door. God put us in our neighborhoods for a reason. God put our neighbors next to us for a reason, as well. Obey God right where you live.

Ok, but HOW do we get better at loving our neighbors?

Sometimes we need a plan to head in the right direction. As you'll hear Brian share on the *The Neighboring Life* DVD, he thought he would be a better dad. Here are a few more details to that story.

The thought of being a better dad had been going through his mind for weeks when his two girls were elementary school age. He wasn't a bad dad. He just imagined he would be better than he was. He realized that good intentions weren't good enough. He needed a plan. Businesses had plans to be profitable. Sports teams had plans on how to win games. He needed a plan to be a better dad. But the plan needed to be simple. It needed to be something easily remembered. So, he came up with three habits he would do regularly for and with his girls. He used words that rhymed so it would be easy to remember them.

The first and most fundamental practice would be to STAY in his girls' world. He admits being wrapped up in his world. Like many of us, Brian's mind was on work. His rest was focused on watching sports. Staying wasn't just about being physically present; it was about being emotionally and mentally present. It was about being a student of his children, learning who God made them to be. It was about listening. It was about being interested. It was about doing things like getting on the floor and playing dolls with them.

The second action was to PRAY for his girls. He did pray for his girls, but he needed to make it even more of a priority. Consistency was key. He immediately discovered he could also pray better by praying more specifically for them because he had practiced staying in their world. He knew what was going on in their lives, so he could be a better intercessor.

The third habit was to speak into their lives, in other words, SAY. He wasn't just to listen but to speak. He wanted to tell them every day he loved them. He wanted to explain to them what Mavis family values are. He wanted them to grow in their understanding of the love of God.

After practicing these for a few weeks, God showed him a habit he had overlooked. Brian and his youngest daughter were goofing around, and she said, "Daddy, my favorite of you is when you're silly!" That's when he realized the importance of regular PLAY. Play is serious business in the life of kids, and it is our loss when we don't also play as adults.

He tweaked the order of the words a bit, and came up with four habits of being a better dad: STAY, PRAY, PLAY, SAY. Brian has found that these habits can be applied to ANY relationship. Use them to deepen your relationships with your kids, parents, siblings, spouse, coworkers, boss, employees, friends, boyfriend, girlfriend, classmates, teammates—anyone in your sphere of influence.

Of course, the focus of *The Neighboring Life* is specifically applied to loving your neighbors—those people who live near you, because we want to get better at what Jesus said matters most. In *The Neighboring Life Launch* you will explore each of these simple practices in greater detail. It is our hope that these practices will move from words on a page to a way of life drawing you closer to God, your family and, of course, your neighbors.

STAY | PRAY | PLAY | SAY

—Excerpt from *The Neighboring Life* Study Guide by Brian Mavis, Rick Rusaw, Kevin Colon and Krista Petty.

Using This Launch Guide

As you prepare for launching *The Neighboring Life* in your church, we want to prepare you with proven strategies to recruit group leaders, connect people into groups, and reach the neighborhoods. While the church members will eventually start groups within their neighborhoods, it's important for them to have the support and encouragement they need through a Neighboring Life small group as they dip their toes into the adventure of neighboring.

But, there is more to this guide than just strategy. Prayer will play a central role in a successful launch. This may go without saying, but an effective launch is empowered by prayer and is not just dependent upon proven strategies. Any strategy that's apart from the power of God is set to fail. But, strategy and prayer together will make for an unstoppable launch into neighboring.

IMPORTANT: The Senior Pastor and Launch Director should review all of the materials in *The Neighboring Life* Launch Guide to see the overall scope of the launch and to begin to think through how to adjust the launch to fit the church context.

Additional launch resources, curriculum and downloads are available at http://www.neighboringlife.com

Launch Overview

We are glad you are joining us in *The Neighboring Life* journey. Our prayer is your community will be transformed as your members love their neighbors well. The members will also see significant change as they slow down and take time for their neighbors. They will learn to serve in personal and practical ways.

STRATEGY OVERVIEW

The Neighboring Life strategy will be:

- **Prayer-Centered**
  Making meaningful decisions by seeking God's will. Praying: Lord, what would you do through me to accomplish your will in my church? Thanking God for blessings and for the opportunity to make a difference in people's lives.

- **Vision-Driven**
  Always clear about a sense of God's calling. What does God want to accomplish in and through the members? Always about people. Creating a culture of growth and maturity as the Church grows up into Christ.

- **Community-Based**
  Authentic sharing and transforming growth occurs in the context of a safe, caring small group setting. The early church followed this model, as Acts 2:46 states: "Every day they continued to meet together in the temple courts. They broke bread in their homes and ate together with glad and sincere hearts."

- **Maximum Impact**
  You will get maximum impact from *The Neighboring Life* launch when everyone in the church participates in each part of the experience. Imagine the excitement when everyone is united—by studying *The Neighboring Life* together and stepping out to practice neighboring in the community.

THE POWER OF ALIGNMENT

Coordinating and aligning the elements of *The Neighboring Life* will impact and produce the kind of spiritual growth that will move the congregation from spectators to active participators in the Body of Christ. Imagine for a moment the impact on the church if every person lived in alignment with God's will in the areas of serving, growing and even giving. What if the people lived in powerful community with their small group or Sunday School class? What if, as groups, people began to experience the power of God in their lives as an entire congregation? By making the most of the following three launch components, you will see the power of God working in the church. These three components build from micro to macro.

1. **Individual Participation**

   This is the real heart of the launch that will produce the greatest spiritual growth among the members of the congregation. The goal is to motivate the congregation to take small steps toward getting to know their neighbors, seeing their neighbors the way that God sees them, and serving their neighbors well. By participating in this launch, each person will be challenged to grow spiritually and experience God's plan for living a transformed life.

2. **Group Participation**

   When we make changes in our lives, we need the support, encouragement and accountability of others. The small group will be the place to both learn the scriptural principles of neighboring as well as trying out neighboring in small, weekly tasks. The group will check in every week to talk about how everyone's first attempts at neighboring worked, what they learned, what they feared, and maybe where they failed. The group is there to celebrate the wins and to cheer everyone on to success in neighboring.

3. **Worship Service Participation**

   The weekend messages will reinforce the neighboring principles as noted in the Companion Guide for *The Neighboring Church*. By hearing about neighboring on the weekend, discussing neighboring in their groups, and practicing neighboring throughout the week, each member will not only learn the principles, but will put them into practice.

The Curriculum

Jesus said, "Love the neighbor as yourself" (Matthew 22:39) Those five words are filled with power, adventure, challenge and so much more. These words, show a way of living this life with others. Those words not only have the power to change others, they have the power to change each participant. And so, they can't dismiss them.

The Neighboring Life **includes:**

- *The Neighboring Life Study Guide* which contains six lessons outlining the principles of neighboring.

- *The Neighboring Life* DVD and streaming video with teaching from Brian Mavis, Rick Rusaw, and others gives the principles to the group as well as shares powerful stories of neighboring.

Casting Vision

The world is changing culturally, politically and even spiritually. As with most organizations, effective ministry over the last 25 years won't look the same as effective ministry over the next 25 years. As Marshall Goldsmith says, "What got us here won't get us there."

The message remains the same. The methods, however, are a different story. While in some communities churches partner with cities to address the greatest needs in their community, not every city is open to these partnerships. But, the greater problem is while the church can serve to meet a physical need by mowing a lawn, painting a fence, or cleaning an alley, often the tasks are disconnected from the relationships with the people who are being served.

Neighboring addresses this issue by encouraging a relationship with one's neighbors first. Then, after people get to know their neighbors and pray for them on a regular basis, they will discover their neighbor's needs and will take steps to help their friend next door rather than a stranger across town. Some have loved their neighbors so well, they find the neighbors inviting themselves to come to church with them.

Connect the church members, attenders, and others to small groups. Launching new groups and connecting the church members to these small groups is a high priority. *The Neighboring Life* launch provides incentive for the congregation to study the Senior Pastor's message more fully in their small groups and Sunday School classes. It provides an opportunity for the Senior Pastor to ask for people to host a new small group or lead a Sunday School class so that everyone can get connected. New group leaders can attract people they already know to be a part of their group—their family, friends, neighbors, coworkers, and others they meet on occasion.

Small Group Ministry Leadership Model

A key factor in launching and sustaining groups is a coaching structure to support the new group leaders. As people attempt to gather their group and lead for the first time, they need someone in their corner to cheer them on. When the new leaders become discouraged because someone they were counting on doesn't join the group or because life just gets in the way, the coach can encourage them to continue and give them perspective like: "It happens to everybody, so don't give up." Knowing they're not alone will go a long way in a successful group launch.

While there is a supervisory aspect of coaching, as Allen White says in *Exponential Groups*, "Coaching is built on a relationship." This relationship will take the new leaders from the moment they say "yes," to the start of their group, through the series, then in their next step study after *The Neighboring Life* study ends.

There will be more discussion on establishing and organizing the Small Group Ministry in the Small Groups and Sunday Schools Team section of this Launch Guide.

Launch Timeline

The timeline keeps the leadership team on track as the launch date gets closer. As much attention should be given to the weeks leading up to the launch as in the series itself. Teams who follow the timeline will have a successful launch.

The Neighboring Life launch can be done any time of the year, but will have the greatest impact in one of three windows on the church calendar:

- **Fall** (between August/September/October and U.S. Thanksgiving)
- **New Year** (between January and Easter)
- **Easter** (between Easter and the end of May)

THINK AHEAD: Even if the launch is months away, start planning early. Gather the leadership team and recruit key roles. The work done in the weeks prior to the launch will affect the success of the launch. Write in your launch date, then populate the dates backward and forward to fill out the rest of the timeline.

WHEN	WHAT	WHO
Week -9	Recruit Launch Director	Senior Pastor
Week -8	Launch Orientation Meeting	Senior Pastor and Launch Team Members
Week -7	Plan Communications Strategy	Communication Team
Week -6	Day of Prayer & Fasting	Prayer Team
Week -5	Group Leader Rally/ Sneak Peek	Group Event Coordinator Senior Pastor
Week -4	Group Leader Recruiting Group Leader Briefing	Senior Pastor Group Training Coordinator
Week -3	Group Leader Recruiting Group Leader Briefing	Senior Pastor Group Training Coordinator
Week -2	Group Leader Recruiting Group Leader Briefing	Senior Pastor Group Training Coordinator
Week -1	Group Connection Event	
Launch Date	**The Neighboring Life Launch • Week 1**	**All**
Week +1	Week 2 • Stay	All
Week +2	Week 3 • Pray	All
Week +3	Week 4 • Play	All
Week +4	Week 5 • Say	All
Week +5	Week 6 • The Neighboring Way of Life	All
Week +6	Celebration	Event Team Coordinator

The Launch Team Overview

No one leader can pull this off by himself/herself. In fact, this is a great opportunity to involve some high capacity leaders in a short-term project which may fit their schedules better than a year-long commitment. Don't just go to the usual suspects or depend solely on the staff. Pray about who God wants on this team, then invite those who come to mind.

The launch team members should not only be committed, but also motivating. As Steve Gladen from Saddleback Church puts it, "The true test of leadership is that leaders have followers." Allow the launch team members to recruit people for their teams. While the task is significant, the relationships are highly important. A title does not make a leader, but influence does.

Details for each Launch Team position are contained in the following pages. These sections will clearly outline the responsibilities as well as the abilities necessary to successfully fulfill the role.

Launch Team Structure
The Launch Team described in this *Neighboring Life Launch Guide* is comprised of a Launch Leader (the Senior Pastor), a Launch Director, and Launch Team Coordinators who, in turn, coordinate a team that carries out one launch task.

No team is perfect, because people aren't perfect. Look for those who can meet at least 40 percent of the qualifications, then get them to work. Chances are they have more ability than anyone initially thought.

At first, hold team meetings monthly. When the team is nine weeks out from the launch, meet every other week. Finally, in the six weeks before the launch and for the six weeks of the study, it might be wise for the Team to meet weekly. Try to have the entire Launch Team assembled well ahead of the launch.

Tactical Considerations

Step-by-step procedures are given for implementing each phase of *The Neighboring Life*. However, remember that these guidelines cannot be simply imposed upon the congregation. Evaluate each recommendation and decide whether it fits the church, factoring in the local context.

Build a strong sense of community within the team. The team needs to get to know each other and share authentically. Praying together, dreaming together, and trusting God together will bond the team together.

Team Descriptions

The Launch Team is described below. Two key positions for overall leadership of the Launch Team are the Senior Pastor and the Launch Director.

Senior Pastor

The Senior Pastor is the key leader in the church. While others have influence, church members will follow the Senior Pastor's direction. If the Senior Pastor leads the way in *The Neighboring Life* launch, the members will get on board. If the Senior Pastor only makes a half-hearted effort, then the church can expect a half-hearted result. But, when the Senior Pastor fully engages in recruiting group leaders, in connecting members into groups, and in leading by example, *The Neighboring Life* launch becomes a powerful tool. For more information on the role of the Senior Pastor, see The Role as Senior Pastor beginning on page 78.

Launch Director

Aligned with the Senior Pastor, the Launch Director will provide overall leadership for the launch. Working with the Senior Pastor, the Launch Director develops the action plan using strategies that meet the goals of the launch, oversees implementation of the action plan, and works with the Senior Pastor to recruit the rest of the Launch Team. In addition, the Launch Director does the following:

- Manages, supports, and provides leadership to each of the Team Coordinators. Coordinates team meetings.

- Manages (along with the Communication Team Coordinator) the overall communication flow for the launch.

- Secures photographers and videographers to record the events of the launch.

- Coordinates with the Communication Team Coordinator for production of print, email, and web materials related to the Launch Director responsibilities.

- Prepares for and submits to an "interview" coordinated by the Communication Coordinator during a weekend service to answer questions about the launch and communicate any needs for volunteers and prayer warriors.

- The Launch Director serves in a very visible role and must be a person who is supportive of and works well with the Senior Pastor. Effective planning and leadership by the Launch Director in the early weeks and months will be crucial to the pacing and success of the launch.

Some of the qualities that are desirable in the Launch Director are:

- Strong leadership gifts.
- Strategic thinking with strong project management skills.
- Well-respected in the church.
- An authentic walk with Jesus.
- Willingness to give the necessary time to this launch.

For more information on the role of the Launch Director, see the Launch Director section beginning on page 86.

Administrative Team Coordinator

The Administrative Team Coordinator is responsible for developing and implementing strategies to support connecting members to small groups and Sunday School leaders; facilitating the distribution of posters, flyers, handouts, email, bulletin inserts, and other communication tools; and working with all Team Coordinators to provide any administrative support needed to make the launch a success. This coordinator:

- Recruits staff and volunteers to help as needed to perform any administrative activities required of the various teams.
- Works with the Communication Team Coordinator to facilitate delivery of print and email messages to individuals, groups, and leadership.
- Coordinates bulletin stuffing (if applicable).
- Distributes materials to coaches, small group leaders, and Sunday School leaders.
- Maintains records on small groups and assists people in getting connected to a new group using software provided by the Launch Director and Small Groups and Sunday School Team Coordinator.

The gifts and skills of the Administrative Team Coordinator should include:

- Good recruitment skills,
- Strong organizational gifts.
- Well-respected among the congregation.
- Knows the internal systems of the church.
- Ability to motivate.
- A good communicator!

Communication Team Coordinator

The launch needs a comprehensive communication plan that includes a broad range of strategies such as video, print, web, email, and signage. The Communication Team Coordinator will identify all points and avenues of communication in the church, produce the needed promotional materials, and oversee the implementation of all communications strategies. In addition, the Communication Team Coordinator does the following:

- Prepares promotional content for the Senior Pastor's pulpit promotion, including video and PowerPoint.

- Recruits a dedicated communications team consisting of members with expertise in the communication mediums of video, print, web, and social media.

- Creates and delivers video promotion materials, graphic designs, printing, and web design for all of the other teams.

- Coordinates Communication Team meetings.

Here's what to look for in the Communication Team Coordinator:

- Strong skills in video production, graphic design, and web production.

- Strong organizational gifts.

- Well-respected among the congregation.

- Knows the internal systems of the church.

- Ability to motivate.

- A good communicator!

For more information on the role of the Communication Team Coordinator, see the Communication Team section beginning on page 91.

Prayer Team Coordinator

The Prayer Team Coordinator implements prayer as a focus for the Launch Team and will develop and implement a prayer strategy throughout all of the church's ministries and age groups for the launch. In addition, the Prayer Team Coordinator does the following:

- Recruits team members to implement the prayer focus and strategy of the launch throughout the church in all age groups and ministries.

- Coordinates with the Communication Team Coordinator for production of printed material, pulpit announcements, email blasts, and signage related to Prayer Team responsibilities.

- Coordinates Prayer Team meetings.

When identifying the Prayer Team Coordinator, here are some characteristics to look for:

- Models a life of, and passion for, prayer.

- Well-respected as a spiritual leader.

- Marked by the character quality of perseverance.

- Can cast vision and motivate people to pray.

- Well-connected to ministry leaders in the church.

For more information on the role of the Prayer Team Coordinator, see the Prayer Team section beginning on page 96.

Small Groups and Sunday School Team Coordinator

One of the most crucial goals of *The Neighboring Life* is to promote group life and assimilate people into small groups or Sunday School classes. This is done by group leaders inviting people they already know and through a Connection event, which takes place at the start of the launch. This can also be done through sign-up opportunities at weekend services, through the web, and other methods the church has available. But, please note, groups formed through signups, websites, or placements create weaker groups that often don't last beyond the launch.

The Small Groups and Sunday School Team Coordinator will recruit the Small Group Ministry team and a sub-team that will develop and implement the plan for the Connection events. In addition, this team coordinator:

- Recruits, develops, and casts vision with a Small Group Ministry team to mobilize and motivate them.

- Recruits and develops a team that implements strategies and plans to orient, train, and lead small group coaches, small group leaders, and Sunday School leaders throughout the entire church for the duration of the launch.

- Trains small group leaders or Sunday School leaders in the use of *The Neighboring Life* small group curriculum.

- Identifies a method for tracking group leadership and membership and works with the Administrative Team Coordinator to implement it.

- Recruits, develops, and casts vision with a Connection Team to mobilize and motivate them.

- Coordinates with the Sunday Worship Team Coordinator regarding facilities needs for the church-wide Connection event.

- Coordinates with the Communication Team Coordinator for production of printed material, pulpit announcements, email blasts, and signage, related to Small Groups and Sunday School Team responsibilities.

- Coordinates the Small Groups and Sunday School Team meetings.

Some qualities to look for in the Small Groups and Sunday School Team Coordinator are:

- A heart for small groups and Sunday School.

- Good relationships with current group leaders.

- Outgoing personality with strategic planning gifts.

- Ability to problem-solve and delegate.

- Ability to recruit new leaders and prepare them to effectively lead their groups.

For more information on the role of the Small Groups and Sunday School Team Coordinator, see the Small Groups and Sunday School Team section beginning on page 103.

Sunday Worship Team Coordinator

The person in this critical role works with the Senior Pastor, Launch Director, and those who plan the worship services in the church will plan special features for weekend services, Connection events, and the Celebration event, if applicable. This person looks for creative ways to help drive home the theme of each week's service. This can be done through testimonies, drama, video, Scripture readings, special music, banners, or numerous other means. This coordinator works with the Senior Pastor to implement and execute these powerful additions to the weekend service. In addition, this person, along with his/her team:

- Develops the Weekend Services Plan using strategies that meet the goals of the launch.

- Coordinates with the Senior Pastor to align sermons with the small group curriculum.

- Coordinates with the Small Groups and Sunday School Team Coordinator regarding facility needs for the church-wide Connection event.

- Organizes and runs the church-wide Connection event.

- Coordinates with the Communication Team Coordinator for production of printed material, pulpit announcements, email blasts, and signage related to Sunday Worship Team responsibilities.

- Coordinates Sunday Worship Team meetings.

Ideally, this person has:

- Good planning gifts and creativity.

- Understanding of the congregation's worship style and what is appropriate in the church's context.

- A heart to assist the Senior Pastor in making the weekend service as effective as possible.

- A commitment to excellence.

FIVE PHASES OF PREPARATION

Below is a sample timeline for the key tasks leading up to the launch.

1. **Orient Themselves**
   - Choose a Launch Director.
   - Familiarize themselves with the launch.
   - Read the Launch Guide.
   - Rally the key leadership.

2. **Set God-Sized Goals**
   - Pray and brainstorm about each area of the launch.
   - Set goals only God can achieve.
   - Order resources from neighboringlife.com

3. **Recruit The Team**
   - Recruit the Launch Team.
   - Pray together.
   - Review the Launch Guide together as a team.

4. **Develop Each Work Group**
   - Each Launch Team coordinator assembles a work group team.
   - Each work group meets for orientation to their task.

5. **Plan and Customize**
   - Evaluate the launch timeline for preparation, promotion, and execution of the launch.
   - Customize the launch for the church.

The Role of the Senior Pastor

Neighboring is a tool God will use to transform your people and your community. As your church members begin to think about their neighbors, they will start thinking less about themselves. Their lives will become more Christ-like. They will be living in obedience to Jesus' command! As their neighbors are loved well, some will visit the church. Others will receive Christ. They will also become the neighbors Jesus imagined.

The Senior Pastor has the most prominent voice in any congregation. The pastor's leadership in this launch is essential to its success. The launch will help members take their weekend into their week. What is taught on Sunday is discussed in the group, then is lived out during the week.

Imagine the congregation in action in the community. See them connect with their neighbors. Witness God using them to learn names, to listen, to pray, and to care for their neighbors. While they are essential practicing outreach and evangelism, those terms shouldn't be used, since many Christians are intimidated by those ideas. But, with the pastor's leadership, members will practice neighboring and actually do outreach and evangelism without those labels.

Leading the Launch

As previously stated, the contribution of the Senior Pastor will make in the launch is to serve as the leader. The launch will not succeed if the pastor is not actively involved in the leadership and vision casting.

The first objective must be to help achieve a sense of ownership of *The Neighboring Life* among the leaders of the church. It is a mistake to assume that approval by the church to participate equals buy-in by leaders and members. Willingness to have a launch does not necessarily signify personal commitment to the launch. Much of the resistance in churches comes when people have not been well informed and when they feel a new idea has been forced upon them. Leadership through influence will go much farther than simply declaring a new direction.

Ask for Prayer

Enlist people to pray for the launch. Ask the elders and leadership of the church to begin praying now. Doing this will cast vision with the leadership and expand the possibilities of who might serve on the team. Also, ask the church leadership to begin asking God to reveal the right people to fill team member roles.

Support the Prayer Team in holding a Day of Prayer and Fasting—a time for all church leadership, launch leadership, and staff to pause and pray for the launch. Do this six weeks before the launch, after the full Launch Leadership Team is in place. Gather the leadership and staff together and ask them to fast and pray on a date you select.

Identify The Launch Director

The Launch Director will align with the Senior Pastor to provide overall leadership for the launch. The Launch Director will work with the pastor to set goals and develop the launch plan using strategies that meet those goals. For more information on the role of the Launch Director, see the section titled Launch Director on page 86.

The Launch Director should be recruited before the initial Launch Orientation Meeting, if possible, so that together you can develop the launch strategies needed for a successful, measurable launch.

Develop Launch Strategies

Read the Launch Overview section beginning on page 69 and work with the Launch Director on developing each of the strategies on the following page:

1. Determine the launch start date. Consider the church calendar dates or holidays when planning the schedule. Then create the Master Timeline to map out the launch.

2. Determine the dates you will hold the Group Leader Briefings and Small Group Connection event. We suggest three consecutive Sundays before the first sermon in *The Neighboring Life* series to recruit hosts and connect people into groups.

3. Set goals and a budget for the launch.

4. Determine if video promotion and/or testimonies will be done to promote the launch during the services.

5. Decide on the structure of the Small Group Ministry.

6. Decide about web signups for group members. If so, consider using a web-based small group tool. Ask the Small Groups and Sunday School Team Coordinator to evaluate current software such as ChurchTeams.com and its online GroupFinder with built-in mapping software. This will allow members to search for a group based on the day, time, and location that work best for them.

7. Decide whether to charge for curriculum up front or simply ask for donations. Be sure to budget for curriculum.

8. Map out the sermons that will be aligned with *The Neighboring Life* small group study using the suggestions found in the Sermon/Text Idea of each lesson in the Companion Guide at the beginning of this book.

9. Be prepared to suggest a next step study for the small groups or Sunday School classes to take following *The Neighboring Life*.

Be on board to:

1. Review the resources at http://www.neighboringlife.com to help you vision cast for *The Neighboring Life*.

2. Maximize the impact of the services by synthesizing the elements of the launch.

3. Sponsor a Launch Orientation Meeting to rally and gain the commitment of the leadership.

4. Gather church staff and leadership to pray for the launch.

5. Cast the vision of the launch for the congregation and promote it from the pulpit.

6. Help recruit small group coaches and follow up with a thank-you to them.

7. Make the invitation for new small group leaders and Sunday School leaders from the pulpit at worship services.

8. Commission new small group leaders and Sunday School leaders during a worship service.

9. During a worship service, invite individuals to embrace the sermon series (that will be aligned with the curriculum) and to join with a small group for the duration of the launch.

10. Promote the Small Group Connection event from the pulpit.

11. Ask current small groups and Sunday School classes to take a break from their current studies to join the launch study.

12. Model the way by leading a group yourself.

13. Celebrate God's work, the small groups, and Sunday School classes at the end of the launch.

Important: The pastor will teach on the curriculum subject the week before the congregation studies the topic in their small groups or Sunday School classes. The expectation is that each small group will study the material the week following the sermon on that subject. The pastor will introduce the next week's theme the next Sunday.

Evaluate and Set Goals

As you begin to set up *The Neighboring Life*, take time to assess where the church currently stands in the following areas and what the church wants to achieve through the launch. Include areas like the number of people involved in:

MINISTRY	CURRENT ATTENDANCE	ATTENDANCE GOAL
Worship Attendance		
Groups and Classes		
Community Involvement		
Ministry		
Leadership Development		

Set The Budget

It is important to set an expectation for the cost of this launch. Below is a budget worksheet to calculate the resource order. Members of the launch team, elders, board members, and other influential leaders should have *The Neighboring Church* book in addition to the *Becoming a Neighboring Church Companion Study and Launch Guide*. All of your current and prospective group and class members should receive their own copy of *The Neighboring Life Study Guide*. Video content should be ordered in a 1:8 ratio (1 DVD/Stream per 8 group members). **Check http://neighboringlife.com for quantity discounts.**

RESOURCE	PRICE	QUANTITY	TOTAL
The Neighboring Church book	$24.99		
Becoming a Neighboring Church Companion Study	$9.99		
The Neighboring Church DVD	$24.99		
The Neighboring Life Study Guide	$9.99		
The Neighboring Life DVD	$24.99		
GRAND TOTAL			

Communicate the Vision for The Congregation

One of the most critical factors affecting the success of the launch is communicating the vision from the pulpit. Through testimonies and stories, the vision can be cast for every member of the congregation. Stories of life-transforming experiences in the individuals have greater impact than any invitation that can be made.

One's own conviction to the benefits of being in a small group are key motivating factors to getting the people to join a small group for the launch. When the pastor says, "I am getting in a group too," the ripple effect is contagious. Everyone wants to "belong." Jump on that bandwagon and use it to draw people in.

People won't grow further than their pastors grow. The Senior Pastor participating in every aspect of the launch will be vital—reading *The Neighboring Church* book, participating in Launch Team meetings, and participating in a small group. When the pastor models God's teaching and lives it out before the congregation, then the congregation will "get it." There is more power in the application of the truths of the sermon to the pastor's own life than there is in any great illustration or eloquent delivery.

Maximize the Impact of Weekend Services

Work closely with the Weekend Worship Team Coordinator to maximize the impact of the services. The worship services during the launch are powerful times that can harmonize the many elements of the launch and underscore the curriculum in a memorable manner. Through the use of several tools designed specifically for the launch, the services will become the time when the power of alignment comes into play by synthesizing the entire launch for the congregation.

Ask people to commit to the launch. Don't discount the power of the pulpit. The pulpit is the rudder that steers the congregation. If there is any time to use the pastor's God-given authority in a way that urges people to spiritual growth, this is that time. Challenge people to jump into the launch with both feet and commit themselves to the principles and the heart of the launch. Foster a holy moment and ask the people to take the big challenge to make a big commitment. People are responsive to a personal challenge.

Pastor's Meetings

We suggest that the pastor sponsors two meetings to kick off the planning and organization of the Launch Team:

1. **Launch Orientation Meeting for Leadership.**
   The first meeting is a dinner meeting for key church leadership, which you could call a "Neighboring Life Orientation Meeting" or a "Neighboring Life Briefing." It is important to secure the commitment of the leadership up front. Hold this meeting at least 6-8 weeks before the first sermon of the series. Commit an entire evening to the meeting so it doesn't feel rushed. In this meeting cast vision for the launch, obtain commitment from the key leaders, and set the stage for a second meeting, described below.

2. **Catch the Vision—Influencers Meeting.**
   This second meeting, held about a week after the first, will include a broader scope of leaders in the church who have direct influence over the majority of the people in the congregation. It will also provide most of the people needed for the Team Coordinator roles (see the Team Descriptions in the Launch Overview section of this Launch Guide for a list of these roles on page 69).

If the Senior Pastor implements this strategy of meeting first with the key leaders and then with the entire team of official and unofficial influencers, it will help create the sense of ownership and commitment that is vital to the success of the church-wide spiritual growth initiative.

The Launch Director

The Launch Director is responsible for recruiting and leading a group of coordinators and other volunteers in pursuit of a successful Neighboring Life Launch. This Launch Guide contains clear guidelines for the roles of the teams.

Aligned with the Senior Pastor, the Launch Director will provide overall leadership for the launch. The Director will develop the action plan using strategies that meet the goals of the launch and will oversee the action plan and work with the Senior Pastor to recruit the rest of the Launch Team. The Director will manage, support, and provide leadership to each of the Team Coordinators. In addition, the Director will:

- Coordinate team meetings.

- Coordinate with the Senior Pastor and Weekend Worship Team Coordinator to align sermons to go along with the small group and Sunday School class curriculum.

- Report progress and challenges to the Senior Pastor and church leadership.

- Be a problem solver. Monitor and encourage all the Team Coordinators and help where necessary.

- Identify and budget for a photographer and/or videographer.

- Manage the overall communication flow for the launch with the Communication Team Coordinator.

- Coordinate with the Communication Team Coordinator for production of print, email, and web materials related to the Launch Director responsibilities.

- Review event planning with the Event Team Coordinator using strategies that will meet the goals of launch.

- Determine the standards and measurements of success and evaluate the success of the launch.

The Launch Director will also work with the Senior Pastor to accomplish the following:

1. Determine the launch start date. Consider the church calendar dates or holidays when planning the schedule.

2. Determine the dates of the Connection event. We suggest three consecutive Sundays to recruit leaders and connect parishioners into groups.

3. Set goals and a budget for the launch.

4. Determine if video promotion and/or testimonies will be done to promote the launch during weekend services.

5. Decide on the structure of the Small Group Ministry. See the Small Groups and Sunday School Team section of this Launch Guide on page 107 for information on a suggested Small Group Ministry Model.

6. Decide about web signups for group members. If so, consider using a web-based small group tool. Ask the Small Groups and Sunday School Team Coordinator to evaluate current software such as ChurchTeams.com and its online GroupFinder with built-in mapping software. This will allow members to search for a group based on the day, time, and location that work best for them.

7. Decide whether to charge for curriculum up front or simply ask for donations. Be sure to budget for curriculum on page 83.

8. Map out the sermons that will be aligned with *The Neighboring Life* small group studies using the suggests found in the Sermon/ Text Idea of each lesson in the Companion Guide at the beginning of this book.

9. Be prepared to suggest next steps for the small groups or Sunday School classes to take following *The Neighboring Life* study.

IMPORTANT: The Senior Pastor will teach on a subject the week before the congregation studies the topic in their small groups or Sunday School classes. The expectation is that each small group will study the curriculum material that week and then the next week's sermon will introduce the next theme.

The Launch Director will recruit the following Team Coordinators:

*   Administrative Team Coordinator

*   Communication Team Coordinator

*   Prayer Team Coordinator

*   Small Groups and Sunday School Team Coordinator

*   Weekend Worship Team Coordinator

*   Special Services Team Coordinator

If the Launch Director works through the Launch Guide, acts in a timely manner, and gets a solid team together, the church should anticipate good results. The effective planning and leadership in these early weeks and months will be crucial to the pacing and success of the launch.

Hold Regular Meetings

After the team has been recruited, hold the first meeting. Communicate the main events timeline to the team and look over this Launch Guide together to become familiar with what lies ahead. At the end of the meeting, spend time sharing the heart for the launch, praying for the team and the launch, and committing to the next meeting date. Spend time in the meeting working on each other's assignments together. This prevents isolation and promotes teamwork and accountability.

Begin holding team meetings right away with whatever team members have been recruited. At nine weeks away from the launch, increase the meeting frequency to every other week. Finally, in the five weeks before the launch and for the six or seven weeks of the launch, it might be wise for the Launch Team to meet weekly.

Touch base with each of the Team Coordinators individually by phone or email every week to encourage, offer help, and pray with the team members.

Communicate the Vision!

Communicate the Senior Pastor's vision for the launch as well as the overall timeline, goals, and budget information with the Team Coordinators.

Each Team Coordinator should be encouraged to carefully review the Launch Overview on page 63 and the segment of this Launch Guide that relates to their area of responsibility. Do this right away!

Choose The Team

In the Launch Overview, you will find descriptions of each of the required Team Coordinators. Write down the names of people who might be the best fit for each role. Pray over each role and choose people with good leadership characteristics.

The Prayer Team's and Small Groups and Sunday School Team's responsibilities take more time than the other coordinator roles. Keep this in mind as the coordinators are selected.

Administrative Team

The Administrative Team is a support team for all the Coordinators to call upon to get administrative tasks done. In addition, this team will order curriculum, disseminate email, handout materials, coordinate bulletin stuffing, keep records on small groups, and connect individuals with groups. Work with the Administrative Team Coordinator to see that these needs are accommodated.

Communication Team

Work with the Communication Coordinator and other Team Coordinators to design the overall church communication strategy for *The Neighboring Life*. For complete information on the roles and responsibilities of the Communication Team, see the Communication Team section on page 91 of this Launch Guide.

Prayer Team

Work with the Prayer Team Coordinator to encourage and monitor the Prayer Team progress toward covering *The Neighboring Life* Launch in prayer. The importance of this cannot be underestimated if the launch is to be God-centered, as it should be. The management of the day-to-day tasks required to carry out the prayer emphasis will fall to the coordinator.

For complete information on the roles and responsibilities of the Prayer Team, see the Prayer Team section on page 90 of this Launch Guide.

Small Groups and Sunday School Team

The Small Groups and Sunday School Team will need encouragement and guidance more than any other single team, as this team's responsibilities are great. This team will identify small group coaches, small group leaders, and Sunday School leaders. They will train and encourage them, provide for curriculum and other resources, and coordinate and monitor promotion of the small group Connection events.

For complete information on the roles and responsibilities of the Small Groups and Sunday School Team, see the Small Groups and Sunday School Team section on page 103 of this Launch Guide.

Weekend Worship Team

The weekend services leading up to and during *The Neighboring Life* are powerful tools that can be used to pull together the many elements needed to drive the message home in an effective manner. The weekend services will see the power of alignment come into play by synthesizing the entire experience for the church and community. The task as Launch Director will again be to encourage the team and monitor progress.

Special Services Team

The Celebration Sunday event is the culmination of *The Neighboring Life* and a celebration of the life changes among the people. Celebration Sunday will be the celebration of what God has done. No matter what elements are built into the Celebration, this is an occasion to get the whole church family together in one place, at one time, and celebrate!

The Communication Team

The Communication Team will be pivotal in overseeing the production and delivery of each piece of communication for the launch. The launch needs a comprehensive communication plan that could include a broad range of strategies such as video, pulpit announcements, bulletin inserts, bulletin announcements, response cards, email, flyers, banners and signage, and promotional postcards. The Communication Team Coordinator will identify all points and avenues of communication in the church, produce the needed promotional materials, and oversee the implementation of all communications strategies. In addition, the Communications Coordinator will:

- Coordinate with the Senior Pastor, Launch Director, and Weekend Worship Team to implement weekend service strategies.

- Prepare content for pulpit promotion, including video and slides.

- Recruit a dedicated Communications Team consisting of members with expertise in the mediums of video, print (bulletin, handout, signage, email), and web.

- Create and deliver video promotion materials, graphic design, printing, and web design for all of the other launch work groups.

- Coordinate Communication Team meetings.

How to Communicate the Launch

One of the challenges for the Communication Team is to adequately and thoroughly communicate the launch to the church family and community. When people don't understand something, they're more likely to be critical.

There are several key components in *The Neighboring Life*, and it will be the responsibility of the team to prepare the materials to inform, promote, and motivate the congregation to be involved.

TACTICAL PRINCIPLES FOR COMMUNICATION

Principle 1.

It doesn't have to be flashy, expensive, or high-tech to grab attention.

Without being elaborate or lavish, the communication can be well done and have a professional feel to it. Be clear in what is communicated, but also be creative. As a team, get everyone's heads together and think of fun, diverse, unexpected ways that can communicate this launch to the congregation. Think outside the box. Brainstorm. Start with this question: If we couldn't use our weekly bulletin, the pulpit, or a newsletter, what would be the most effective ways to communicate this launch to our people?

Warning: As the team gets creative, don't lose the clarity of the message. When introducing something new, it is more important to be clear than clever. Remember, the goal is for people to get the information, not to be impressed with the creativity.

Principle 2.

Find as many times and ways to communicate as possible.

One widely known law of advertising is that a message must be communicated seven times before it really sinks in. One of the dangers is to assume that because the team is familiar with something, others are also. When the team thinks it is communicating adequately, double the efforts. Remember, you cannot over-communicate!

Principle 3.

Clear the path for *The Neighboring Life* to succeed.

If this launch really is the start of church's long-term initiative into neighboring, then ensure it receives proper priority in the church communication. The clutter must be cleared. All groups in the church should know the dates for the launch and make necessary adjustments.

Principle 4.

Communication is not just an activity. It is an attitude.

One of the most effective communication devices at the disposal is the leadership team's attitude. It is imperative that the Senior Pastor, the Launch Team, and the Communication Team have a contagious enthusiasm for what is coming. It is crucial for the Senior Pastor to champion the launch from the beginning. As the Senior Pastor demonstrates and talks about his or her own commitment and involvement, the value of the launch rises. Don't be afraid to utilize the weekend services to ask for commitment and participation from the congregation.

BUILDING THE TEAM

The communications strategy is carried out by a Communications Team using contact points throughout the congregation. The team consists of people with gifts and skills in communications, and the contact points include liaisons and email.

Team Size: This is definitely not a one-person job. The size of the team will vary depending on the size of the church. Get as many people as feasible to spread the workload, but not so many that it becomes complicated to manage.

Team Member Skills: Select team members who bring a good working knowledge of various communication mediums like print, video, web, social media and email. Team members should understand all segments of the church and the existing communication avenues that are used, if possible.

Pray

Encourage the team to pray at every opportunity during the planning and execution of the events of the launch.

Build a Communication Strategy

The Coordinator is necessary to accomplish the task of communicating the launch to the church and community. Establish a communication liaison in each of the Launch Teams. This will likely be the Team Coordinator or a designee. These liaisons will be the contacts for communicating with each team. This will assure communication throughout the Launch Team.

We recommend the use of a multi-tiered communications strategy that employs a combination of verbal, written, and graphic tools to keep people informed about the events of the launch.

The communications strategy may use more bulletin announcements, inserts, or handouts, or it might be helpful to use all communications avenues. It is advisable for you to lay out all the bulletin announcements, handouts, and bulletin inserts, and coordinate them with the pulpit announcements for each week, then decide what the best communications options will be.

Communicating with the Congregation

At the beginning of the launch, it is important to give people ample opportunity to understand what the church is doing and why. Don't worry about talking about the launch too much. The more it's communicated, the more people will become interested and feel comfortable with some new concepts.

Video:
> Consider using video testimonies or movie clips to help bring home the message in the weekend services.

Web:

Build a web page to promote the launch. Determine what design is needed for the launch and how it will accommodate both new leader and member signups for groups, if applicable. Web strategy ideas include:

- Post all information on the website to announce events, themes, and prayer requests.

- Research other church small group websites for ideas.

- Enable online small group sign up (like the online GroupFinder software on ChurchTeams.com).

Distribution Methods

In addition to the communication strategies listed above, the Communications Team already has the two most important communication tools needed: networks of relationships and existing communication channels. Work hard to identify all the various ways that information gets communicated in the church. Many ministries have developed their own systems of communicating with their people. Tap into the current systems and maximize their use.

Work with the Administrative Team for the distribution of the materials. They are standing by with volunteers ready to stuff bulletins, send email announcements, and staff an Information Table. Make handouts available at an Information Table after they are initially distributed or point them to the Launch website, in case people missed them.

The Administrative Team should start collecting all the email addresses in the church right away. While email communication shouldn't be the only means of communication, it is a quick and efficient means of keeping in touch with a significant portion of the congregation. Work with the Administrative Team to have emails sent out.

The Prayer Team

The success of *The Neighboring Life* Launch is not built merely on strategy. It must be built on a foundation of prayer. Doing God's work without God's power is fruitless. Every aspect of the preparation and the launch must be covered in prayer.

The Prayer Team will consist of a dedicated group committed to praying for the church-wide Neighboring Life Launch and to getting everyone involved in praying for the launch. The objective is to pray for God's will and acknowledge that, with His power and strength, all things can be accomplished.

Prayer Team Coordinator

As the Prayer Team Coordinator, the job is to implement prayer as a focus for *The Neighboring Life* experience. In addition, the coordinator will:

*   Recruit team members to implement the prayer focus and strategy of the launch throughout the church in all age groups and ministries. If the church currently has a prayer team, then enlist those members into this effort.

*   Coordinate with the Communication Team Coordinator for production of printed materials, pulpit announcements, and email blasts related to Prayer Team responsibilities. Set up separate prayer sessions to support the goals of the church-wide small group launch.

*   Coordinate Prayer Team meetings and distribute a prayer list weekly.

*   Attend and lead prayer in Launch Team meetings, when possible.

The Priority of Prayer
"Whenever God determines to do a great work, he first sets his people to pray."
—C.H. Spurgeon

Declare the church's need and dependence upon God. Looking ahead to the scope of *The Neighboring Life* Launch can be overwhelming. It can lead to feelings of inadequacy, fear or stress. Let God use those feelings to bolster the faith and confidence in him.

View prayer as the centerpiece of preparation for the launch. In order for prayer to be the centerpiece of the preparation for *The Neighboring Life* Launch, it must be a central focus for the entire team, not just the Prayer Team. There are many tasks to be accomplished over the next few months to prepare for this small group launch. Don't forget that perhaps the single most important preparation is that which takes place in the quietness of the prayer closet. Those who lead this experience must prepare personally through prayer.

Be aware of these prayer deterrents:

- Allowing urgent tasks and meetings to crowd out what's important.
- Following good intentions without a plan.
- Viewing prayer as nice but not necessary.
- Dry, mechanical, passionless prayer.
- Lack of modeling from leadership.
- Lack of perseverance and faith.

Just Do It!

Churches are filled with people who do not need more training on prayer. They just need to pray. Churches need a Nike strategy—JUST DO IT! This is not about having prayer meetings where 45 minutes are spent sharing prayer requests and then three minutes are spent in prayer. Rather, this is about getting serious in prayer and calling upon God to do a great work. Serious doesn't necessarily mean extended periods of time in prayer. It means to pray often and regularly, which could end up being extended periods of time in prayer.

A NOTE TO THE PRAYER TEAM

Don't take these instructions as heaping guilt on the prayer team or the people. Christians often have feelings of inadequacy or failure when it comes to our prayer lives. Prayer can be marginalized by long meetings, endless tasks, and mounting deadlines. Even good intentions can soon turn to regret. Everyone can learn much about prayer, so be proactive about becoming people of prayer. One goal of this Neighboring Life Launch is to deepen the church's faith and faithfulness in prayer.

Seize every opportunity to pray:

- Spend significant time during the meetings in prayer.
- Gather a handful of people before or after a weekend service to pray.
- Pray in the small group or Sunday School class.
- Pray when you have a few minutes alone: in the car, at lunch, before going to sleep, or just after waking.
- Pray as you drive through your neighborhood.

The possibilities are limitless. You don't need extra meetings to have a strong focus on prayer.

Lead by Modeling

Prayer is more caught than taught.

- Commit to more prayer time personally.
- Talk about prayer, and its value, to others.
- Be excited about the difference that prayer can make.
- Challenge and enlist others to pray.

BUILDING THE TEAM

1. **Invite the core Prayer Team members.**
   - Form an extended prayer team of current ministry leaders and volunteers to pray for *The Neighboring Life* Launch on a regular basis.
   - Consider the current prayer warriors in the church.
   - Get a list of neighborhoods from a local realtor and pray over each neighborhood by name.

2. **Motivate ministry leaders to pray for *The Neighboring Life* Launch.**
   - Host a Day of Prayer and Fasting for the church staff, Launch Team, and ministry leaders. Ask the Senior Pastor to assemble the people for this.
   - Ask the Senior Pastor to periodically gather the staff to pray for *The Neighboring Life* launch.
   - Provide small group leaders and Sunday School leaders with weekly prayer requests.
   - Ask the pastors and leaders to visit small groups and Sunday School classes to pray with them about *The Neighboring Life* Launch.

3. **Motivate the entire church to pray for *The Neighboring Life* Launch.**
   - Hold a church-wide prayer event.
   - Use vision dinners, training sessions, and every opportunity to request prayer.
   - Hold a weekly prayer meeting on the church campus.
   - Use visual reminders for people to pray.
   - Motivate current small groups and Sunday School classes to pray for the launch.
   - Motivate individuals to get a prayer partner for *The Neighboring Life*.

4. **Disseminate prayer requests and prayer meeting reminders.**
   - Gather prayer requests from the Launch Teams and hand them out to the church staff, Launch Team members, and ministry leaders.
   - Use bulletin announcements, PowerPoint, and pulpit announcements.
   - Use email and prayer venues that already exist in the church.

5. **Ask the Senior Pastor to pray from the pulpit.**
   - Pray for the launch leadership.
   - Pray for the commissioning of the small group and Sunday School leaders as they launch new groups.

Hold Regular Meetings

After the team has been recruited, hold the first meeting. Communicate the main events timeline to the team and look over this Launch Guide together to get on track. At the end of the meeting, spend time sharing the vision for the launch, praying for the team and the launch, and committing to the next meeting date. Begin holding weekly team meetings right away with whatever team members have been recruited.

The Plan for Prayer in the Launch

As a Prayer Team, begin to carefully consider some of the following questions:

- What are the needs of our congregation that we can pray for?
- What are we asking God to do in us and in our church during *The Neighboring Life* Launch?
- How can we pray for our Senior Pastor and the other leaders in our church?

- What are some strategies that could help pockets of people throughout our congregation engage in prayer for the launch?

- What are we trusting God for that is God-sized?

- Use the following checklists as a guide to develop ideas for infusing prayer into the structures of the church in preparation for and throughout *The Neighboring Life* Launch. Check the ideas that would work in the church setting, and write more ideas in the blank spaces.

Launch Team Strategy

- Hold a Day of Prayer and Fasting, a time for all church leadership, launch leadership, and staff to pause and pray for the launch. Do this about four weeks before the launch after the full Launch Leadership Team is in place. Gather the leadership and staff together and ask them to fast and pray on a designated date.

- Email or hand out a weekly prayer update with new requests each week.

-

Corporate Strategy

- Using a church-wide prayer focus, place prayer verses and prayer requests in the bulletin or online each week.

- Hold prayer times before, during, and after weekend and midweek services. Use prayer testimonies in weekend services to encourage prayer.

-

Small Groups and Sunday School Class Strategy

- Place a Prayer Tent Card in plain view at each meeting to remind the group to pray for *The Neighboring Life* Launch.

- Ask small groups and Sunday School classes to dedicate five to ten minutes each week to prayer for *The Neighboring Life* Launch.

- Pray each week for *The Neighboring Life* Launch activities and results.

- Have each group adopt one *Neighboring Life Launch* team member to pray for (by name or function).

-

Individual Strategy

- Distribute the Prayer Reminder Cards to the congregation to remind them to pray through Neighboring Life Launch goals and objectives.

- Commit to praying daily for *The Neighboring Life* Launch.

- Find a prayer partner to meet with at least weekly to pray for *The Neighboring Life* Launch.

-

"There is no power like that of prevailing prayer. It turns ordinary mortals into men of power. It brings power. It brings fire. It brings rain. It brings life. It brings God."
—Samuel Chadwick

The Small Groups and Sunday School Team

This launch is about surrounding people with support as they take their first steps into neighboring. While groups can meet a number of significant needs in the church like connection, discipleship, and serving, the idea of neighboring will be new to a lot of people and possibly scary or intimidating to them. First steps in neighboring should be celebrated in groups. Groups can also supply the subtle accountability of knowing someone will ask how each member's assignment went the previous week.

The Small Groups and Sunday School Team Coordinator will assume the role of Small Group Ministry Leader for the launch. The key roles, initially, are:

- Recruiting the team.
- Praying for the team.

The key tasks for the launch are:

- Recruiting Coaches who can provide support and direction to a group of small group leaders or Sunday School leaders. Experienced leaders are a great resource to coach new leaders.

- Recruiting small group leaders and/or Sunday School leaders. While the Senior Pastor will make general invitations for the church to lead groups, the team will be responsible for also recruiting people individually to lead groups.

- Connecting small group leaders and Sunday School leaders with a Coach and connecting coaches with the Small Group Team.

- Recruiting two key team members: the Connection Event Coordinator and the Leader Training Coordinator. Each of these leaders will need to build their own teams to manage their respective tasks as described later in this section.

- With the help of the Communication Team Coordinator, developing promotional strategies and materials to promote events (the Connection event, Leader Orientations, and team meetings).

- With the help of the Administrative Team, distributing promotional materials and small group curriculum, and keeping records for all tiers of the Small Group Ministry (coaches, small group leaders, and group member assignments).

Building The Team

The make-up of the Small Groups and Sunday School Team will be more varied than some of the other teams in the launch because there are a few major thrusts to manage:

- Building the Small Group Ministry by recruiting coaches, and small group and Sunday School leaders, if needed.

- Connecting new group members with small groups and Sunday School classes by encouraging new leaders to gather their own groups, by hosting a Connection event, and providing onsite, web, and other opportunities for people to sign up for groups (if necessary).

- Recruit a coordinator to manage this function as defined in the Connection Coordinator section below.

- Resourcing and training new and existing leaders throughout the launch. Recruit a coordinator to manage this function as defined in the Training for Leaders section below.

To handle these initiatives, the team should have a variety of people who collectively possess a combination of these skills:

- A heart for small groups and Sunday School classes for adults.

- Ability to recruit new small group leaders and Sunday School leaders.

- Good relationships with current leaders of small groups and Sunday School classes.
- Ability to prepare small group leaders to effectively lead their groups.
- Event planning and implementation skills.
- Training skills.
- Ability to influence and inspire.

Involvement Builds Success

Inviting people to play relatively small, but important, roles on the team increases energy, passion, knowledge, networking, creativity, influence, and ownership of the mission. Providing focused tasks, comprehensive training, and a wide variety of resources encourages volunteers to have a good experience and to perform their respective roles successfully.

The Team

The two key team leaders are a Connection Event Coordinator and a Leader Training Coordinator. Each of these leaders will need to build their own teams to manage their respective tasks.

The key tasks for the Connection Event Coordinator are:

- To connect small group and Sunday School leaders with a coach and to host the Connection event to connect members to small groups.
- To provide onsite, web, and other opportunities for people to sign up for groups and connect new group members with small group and Sunday School leaders.

The key tasks for the Leader Training Coordinator are:

- To resource and support new and existing groups throughout the launch.
- To conduct leader orientations and training.
- To support and encourage small group and Sunday School leaders with events and communication.

In the space below, write down the names of people who would best fit each of these roles. Pray over each role and choose people with the characteristics needed to fulfill the responsibilities of these roles.

Connection Event Coordinator: _____

The person in this role will build a team to develop the plan and oversee the implementation of the many elements of connecting people into small groups and Sunday School classes, including the Connection event.

Leader Training Coordinator: _____

The person in this role will build a team to facilitate orientation and training of small group and Sunday School leaders for adult groups.

Once the team leaders have been identified, set to work building each team.

HOLD REGULAR MEETINGS

After recruiting the team, hold the first meeting. Communicate the main events timeline to the team and look over this Launch Guide together to get everyone on track. At the end of each meeting, spend time sharing the vision for the launch, praying for the team and the launch, and committing to the next meeting date. Spend time in the meeting working on each other's assignments together. This prevents isolation and promotes teamwork and accountability.

Begin holding monthly team meetings right away with whatever team members have been recruited. At nine weeks out from the launch, meet every other week. Finally, at five weeks before the launch and for the six to seven weeks of the launch, meet weekly.

Pray

Encourage the team to pray at every opportunity during planning and executing the events of the launch.

Small Group Ministry Leadership Model

Developing a structure for leading the church's Small Group Ministry is an essential element in sustaining the small group movement in the church post-launch. Coaches will oversee up to 4-5 new small group leaders each, while they continue to lead their own groups. The coach will help fulfill the mission of the church by

1. managing, ministering, and administering to the spiritual development of individuals

2. encouraging the growth and expansion of their four or more small groups.

Under this model, coaches build relationships with the leaders in their care. This may involve disseminating information to the Small Group Ministry leadership and answering any questions or concerns within groups that the small group leader is unable to handle. A coach is usually selected from individuals who have demonstrated leadership skills inside or outside the church and are committed to the principle of doing small group life together. The most important qualification is that coaches actually care about their role and the leaders they serve. They cast vision for the community and are the shock absorbers--solving issues and problems as they arise.

The position of coach helps fulfill the mission of the church by managing, ministering to, and administering the spiritual development of individuals and by insuring the growth and expansion of the small groups under them. The role of coach is further defined on the following page.

Connect with leaders regularly through:

- One-on-one meetings.

- A group visit (at least once during the launch).

- A weekly phone call.

- An occasional email to encourage or train leaders (email should not be the primary means of communication between coaches and group leaders).

SMALL GROUP AND SUNDAY SCHOOL LEADER ROLE FOR THE LAUNCH

Purpose:
Someone interested in gathering a group of friends to launch *The Neighboring Life* together. Leader requirements may vary from church to church.

Responsibilities:
- Bring a group of people together to connect with each other and to cultivate authentic relationships with one another (Hebrews 10:24–25. Ephesians 2:19).

- Affirm what the leader sees God doing in the lives of the member. Challenge them to next steps in neighboring (Colossians 1:28. Ephesians 4:15).

- Train the members for ministry by giving every person a role or responsibility that helps mobilize them into ministry both inside and outside the group. The leaders should ask the group to take responsibilities in the group like bringing refreshments, hosting the group in their home, or leading the discussion. Of course, every group member will be challenged to get to know their neighbors, to pray for their neighbors, and to serve their neighbors as opportunities present themselves (Ephesians 4:11–13. 1 Corinthians 12:7. 1 Peter 3:10).

- Challenge group members in the area of SAY by practicing how to tell their story and by supporting group members as they pray about sharing their story with their neighbors (Matthew 28:18–20. Acts 20:24. 2 Timothy 2:2).

- Sustain them spiritually by gathering them together for worship, prayer, devotions and communion, if appropriate. (Romans 12:1–2. 1 Corinthians 15:58).

Small Groups or Sunday School?

It doesn't matter which meeting format is used as long as there is heart-to-heart interaction. Both small groups and Sunday School classes are places to discover the neighboring life. Remember the goal is to engage church members in neighboring, not to convert groups and classes over to the same meeting style. Introduce neighboring within a familiar group or class context rather than attempting to change the format. The key change is a move toward neighboring, not a move from Sunday School classes to groups.

Embracing *The Neighboring Life* in Small Groups and Sunday School Classes:

Small Groups	Sunday School Classes
Allow for longer fellowship time.	Convenient schedule-wise.
Are more conducive to community.	Convenient location.
Have an infinitely expandable structure.	Provides childcare.
Demonstrate good stewardship—using homes so church facilities are not used.	Easier to supervise leaders.
Are more likely to attract new people and neighbors.	

Identifying and Recruiting Small Group and Sunday School leaders

Start by praying and asking God to reveal potential leaders. Jesus said, "Ask the Lord of the harvest to send out workers into His harvest field." Matthew 9:38

CAUTION: You might conclude that starting 5, 10, or 20 new groups isn't possible because there isn't room in the building. Let this be a faith-stretching moment. Begin to think outside the box. Don't limit the options to the current times the groups meet or limit them to the church building. Pastor Rick Warren of Saddleback Church says, "Don't let the shoe tell the foot how big it can get."

Don't let the building determine how many groups you can start. For adult groups, think of other places the groups could meet—offices, homes, or anywhere a video can be viewed.

POSSIBLE GROUP LEADER CANDIDATES

1. **Key Leaders.**
    Look among the current church staff and key leaders serving in existing roles that might be willing to lead a group. It's a great opportunity to get some of the long time leaders on the front lines of ministry with some unconnected people.

2. **Current Small Group Leaders.**
    Encourage existing group hosts to open their groups to new members for the launch.

3. **Current Small Group Members.**
    Encourage existing group hosts to release people from their group to start a group for the 6 week series. Since they have experience

in group life, they are great candidates.

4. **Current Participants in Ministries.**
   Look around in the church. Consider those who serve on committees, who are ushers or greeters, or those who work with missions or outreach. People who serve already can be relied on to understand and promote the value of community for at least a short-term experience.

5. **Core Church Members.**
   These people may not have an official leadership title, but they are involved and faithful.

6. **Pulpit Invitation.**
   Ask the Senior Pastor to

   • Invite existing small group leaders or Sunday School leaders to commit to the launch

   • Make a call for new small group leaders during his or her sermons for the three weeks prior to the launch.

Make sure you have New Leader Commitment Cards available either in the bulletin or as a handout for people to fill out and turn in during the service. If an electronic method would be a better option, consider a text to signup option or an online survey tool with a mobile format. The key is to have the leader signup take place **in the service**—not in the lobby, and definitely not at home.

Connection Event.
The small group leader and Sunday School leader Connection event is a catalytic event during the launch that will bring the people together to join short-term groups. While personal invitation by the group leader is the best method for connecting people into groups, the Connection event serves as an environment for prospective group members to meet

the group leaders face to face and then sign up for a specific group. The Connection event will hopefully prevent people from falling through the cracks during the group signup. The Connection event should replace the need for an online group signup or group placement process.

HOW TO CREATE NEW GROUPS
(Taken from a blog post on allenwhite.org.)

Many methods of connecting people into groups fail. They don't create lasting connections, which means every time groups are launched, pastors are recruiting new leaders and connecting people to new groups. Here's how this usually goes:

Step 1.
A prospective group member turns in a sign up card, or requests a group on the church's website, or selects a group from a small group directory.

Step 2.
The church staff must either place the person in a group or send their information to the leader of an open group.

Step 3.
The group leader may or may not contact the prospective member.

Step 4.
If the prospective members are contacted, they may or may not show up to the group.

Step 5.
If the prospective members show up for the group, they may or may not continue with the group.

Step 6.
The Small Group Pastor/Director becomes very frustrated.

At least this is how it's gone in many churches. Typically, each step down the list cuts the previous number in half—100 people sign up, then 50 are contacted, then 25 show up to a group, and then 12.5 continue with the group. Talk about diminishing returns!

But, this isn't the worst of it.

So, how do churches connect people into groups if signup cards, websites, and directories don't work very well?

1. **Everyone who has friends should start a group.**

   "Everyone is already in a group." That's the first sentence in *Exponential Groups* by Allen White. People have friends, neighbors, co-workers, relatives, and others they can do a study with. The people in any church are already connected. They just need some direction in intentionally doing something about their spiritual growth. An easy to use curriculum and an experience leader to coach them will take these leader-friends a long way in developing a "small group."

2. **If they don't want to "lead"...**

   Then, they should join the group led by their friend. Personal invitation is an amazing tool for connecting people into lasting groups. Even groups who will be open to new members should start with the leader personally inviting people.

   Now, if someone who wants to lead a group but expects the church to give them a group, they probably have a teaching gift and need a class to instruct. This will not make for a good small group. Encourage them to bring together their own group.

3. **If they don't have friends...**

   Some folks are new to the community or new to the church, and they legitimately don't know anybody. How do they get in a group? If they don't know anyone, they can't invite people, and they won't get invited. Now what?

   This is where the Connection event comes in. This is an Open House environment at the church where prospective members can meet group leaders face to face. They may recognize the leader from somewhere or vice versa. At a minimum, they get a sense of whether or not the leader is someone they want to hang out with for the next 6 weeks. Once they've decided, the prospective members sign up for the specific group they want to be a part of. No cards. No cold calls. The relationship has started. They know whose house they're going to, and the leader knows who's coming.

Final Instructions

Efficient means of connecting people are not the same as effective means. Usually a task-oriented approach to forming relationally-based groups falls short. Forget group formation as a task. By forming groups in a relational way, groups will outlast how you were forming groups previously.

Rallying The Current Leaders

The first step to take when starting to recruit leaders for the new groups you want to form for *The Neighboring Life* is to hold a Leader Rally or Sneak Peek event. Invite existing leaders and their apprentices or co-leaders.

The purpose of the meeting is to gain buy-in for the events of the launch and give leaders a heads-up about what is coming. This will be the time to encourage leaders to put their current studies on hold for the launch and open their groups to new people. When inviting hosts and leaders to the Rally, ask them to bring the prospective leaders in their groups to the meeting as well.

Expanding Existing Groups

Existing small group leaders are encouraged to expand their groups for the duration of the launch. Small group leaders can make a list of friends, family, co-workers, neighbors, and others who might be interested in the study. Ask each leader to write down the names and pray over who to invite.

Small Group Management and Recordkeeping

The church will benefit from a software solution for tracking the Small Group Ministry information. If you already have a software solution in place, great! If not, work with the Connection Event Coordinator and Administrative Team Coordinator to evaluate current software such as ChurchTeams.com.

Once the processes are in place, the Coordinator should work with the Administrative Team Coordinator to track the Small Group Ministry leaders, small group leaders, and members for small group sign-up and management.

Tools

Curricula: *The Neighboring Life* curriculum comes in two parts: a study guide for each group member and a video component (DVD or streaming media) for use in the group meetings.

About the Authors

BRIAN MAVIS is the President of America's Kids Belong and former Pastor of Community Transformation at LifeBridge Christian Church. Brian was the first General Manager of SermonCentral.com from 2000-2005. He has written curriculum for campaigns including Bono's *One Sabbath Campaign*, Mel Gibson's *Passion of the Christ*; World Vision's *Faith in Action* and *The Hole in Our Gospel*. Brian co-authored *The Neighboring Church* along with Rick Rusaw. Brian and his wife, Julie, have two daughters and reside in Windsor, CO.

RICK RUSAW is the Senior Pastor at LifeBridge Christian Church. He is co-author of several books including *The Neighboring Church*, *The Externally Focused Church, The Externally Focused Quest, The Externally Focused Life,* and the *Life on Loan* series. Prior to LifeBridge, Rick served as a Vice President at Cincinnati Christian University. Rick and his wife, Diane, have three children and five grandchildren and reside in Longmont, CO.

KRISTA PETTY is a connector and story-teller for neighboring and community transformation movements across the U.S. She has served with Leadership Network, LifeBridge Christian Church, Carolina Cross Connection, Simon Solutions, and many others. Krista and her husband, Steve, live in Spirit Lake, IA and have three children and two grandsons.

Allen White is the author of *Exponential Groups: Unleashing Your Church's Potential*. He is a church consultant specializing in small groups and curriculum development. Allen has created curriculum including *The Daniel Plan Small Group Study* for Rick Warren, the *Intentional Parenting Discussion Guide* with Doug and Cathy Fields, the *Holy Ambition Small Group Study* and video with Chip Ingram, the *Destiny Study Guide* and video for Dr. Tony Evans, and served in various roles on many other curriculum projects. He blogs at allenwhite.org. Allen, his wife, Tiffany, and their four children live in the Greenville, SC area.